ALIEN CREATURES

One of the many
monstrosities of **The
Outer Limits**

Ray Harryhausen's
Venusian Ymir from
**20 Million Miles to
Earth**.

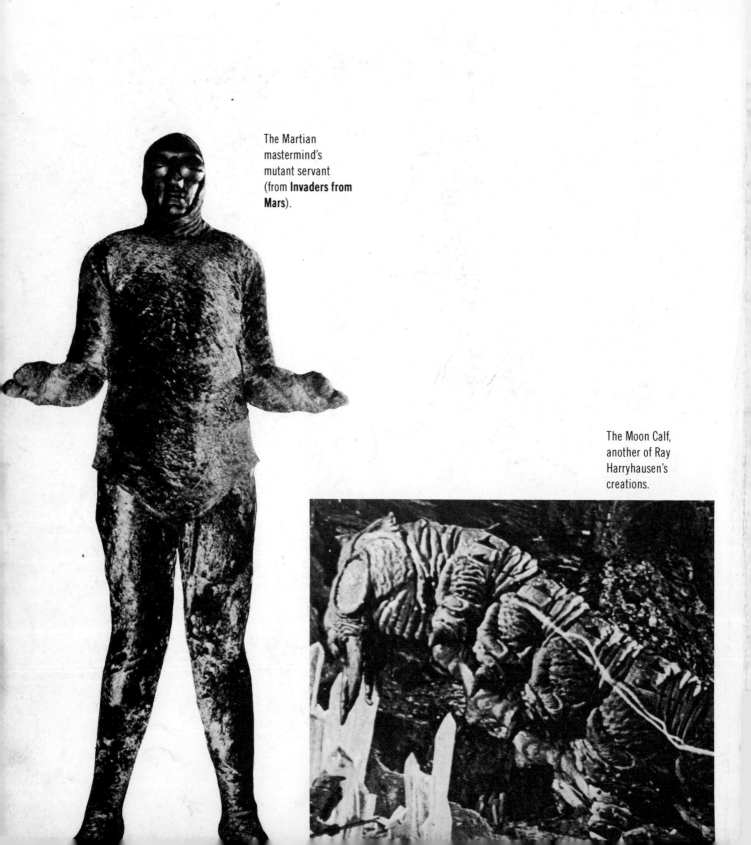

The Martian
mastermind's
mutant servant
(from **Invaders from
Mars**).

The Moon Calf,
another of Ray
Harryhausen's
creations.

INTRODUCTION

Natural History, described beasts that remain peculiar enough to command interest even into the twentieth century, when recognizable versions of some of them can be found shambling or galloping across the plains of Barsoom in Edgar Rice Burroughs' fantasies of the Red Planet. Though Burroughs never quite dared to resurrect the Yale—an antelopelike beast that escapes from predators by hurling itself off high cliffs, making a soft landing on the tips of its long and flexible horns—the author's mastodonlike beasts of burden (which emerge again in a couple of delightfully understated shots in *Star Wars*) could very easily have graced the illuminated pages of the twelfth-century French *Royal Bestiary.* T. H. White's lovely translation informs us that "There is an animal called an Elephant which is unable to copulate." The elephant in question looks, in the familiar phrase, as if it has been designed by a committee similar, in this respect, to Dürer's wonderful armor-plated rhinoceros, obviously drawn from a similar bestiary.

Inasmuch as the bestiaries were compilations of hearsay, misinformation, misunderstanding of classical sources and pious lies set down by cloistered monks who almost certainly had never clapped eyes on the animals they describe, it is amazing how many of the descriptions come near the truth, once allowance has been made for the heavy weight of Christian iconography each beast must bear. It should be remembered that despite their often hilarious inaccuracies the bestiaries were attempts to describe the actual life forms of far places, unlike the narrations of goblins, elves and demons that formed the other side of the medieval tale-teller's repertoire. Already there is a distinction forming between the horror story and the speculative tale of distant lands and strange creatures. Above all, the bestiaries, like science fiction, are expressive of a boundless curiosity about the universe, unlike the horror story in its goblin form, which proclaims from its very first line (preferably uttered in a darkened room with the fire built up and the doors and windows bolted against the night), "Anyone who wants to know anything about what goes on outside this village (town, country, continent, planet) is asking for trouble." Or, to give the phrase its characteristic horror-movie form, "There are some things Man was not meant to know."

The dichotomy created by the warring human urges of curiosity and xenophobia is certainly of far older provenance than the Middle Ages. The Greeks never resolved the difference. On the one hand, they sentenced some humans in their mythology who made the blasphemous attempt to unravel the mysteries proper to the gods alone to punishments more fiendish than anything Ming the Merciless ever dreamed up for the upstart Flash Gordon. But on the other hand, some of the most heroically curious were rewarded with honorary godhood. Indeed, the Greek pantheon itself, teetering between serene omniscience and childish spitefulness, remains a powerful figure for the divided nature of human feelings concerning that which transcends everyday experience. The gods are wise, but they are not compassionate in the human sense

Saturn, the vengeful deity, devours his children. From a painting by Francisco Goya.

INTRODUCTION

A Matthias Grünewald beastiary from his painting of the "Temptation of Saint Anthony."

of the word. Or, conversely, they are benevolent according to their lights (which are beyond our ken), but they care little for human wisdom. Either way they are profoundly Other, and in that sense they can be seen as the ancestors of the most maturely conceived science-fiction extraterrestrials. Apollo, like the mysterious builders of the monoliths in *2001: A Space Odyssey,* involves himself in human affairs solely for reasons of his own, and human speculation about his motives must necessarily remain idle. Instead, the pious Greek adopted an attitude of resignation, bowing before the mystery of the gods' ambiguous existence and submitting to their unguessable plan. Similarly, open-minded resignation in the face of alien mystery is a deep theme in serious science fiction and the best of the science-fiction films. Books such as Arthur C. Clarke's *Childhood's End* and movies like *Close Encounters of the Third Kind* suggest that the moment we accept the motives of the godlike aliens as sufficient unto themselves we will, as it were, pass a test and become eligible for godhood ourselves.

The characteristic urge to discover something or someone beyond human frailty who can explain us to ourselves is the wellspring of all religion. But it is a mark of the smugness of our species that we tend to portray the gods in human form. Anubis may wear the head of a jackal, but his body is that of a man. The unimaginable formless form of the Holy Spirit reaches us through the human body of the Son of Man.

INTRODUCTION

Even the ineffable ground of all being, union with which is the meditative goal of the siddhas and Zen mystics, finds a concrete human image in the smile on the lips of Gautama. And as religious images secularize to become the Others who visit us in science-fiction films and books—figures of popular entertainment, certainly, but products of the same human yearning after answers that summoned up the gods—they too are presented in the nature and often the exact form of humankind.

Klaatu in *The Day the Earth Stood Still* is only humanity raised to the tenth power, mysterious, perhaps, gifted with great wisdom, but still killable. And he brings us a warning about our hubristic behavior much as the angel appeared to Jacob in human form to wrestle him out of his preconceptions. Even when the make-up artists take hold to create the most frightful Bug-eyed Monsters they can imagine, the end product is usually anthropoid in essence.

It may be argued that the man shape is retained in the low-budget science-fiction movies precisely because they are low-budget: It's certainly cheaper to put an actor in an alien suit than it is to animate a creature with a totally alien shape. Yet even with $18 million to play

A 1621 engraving shows a bizzare interpretation of the whale assisting in the discovery of the New World.

with, Steven Spielberg, director of *Close Encounters of the Third Kind*, finally chose to model his aliens along human lines.

The reasons behind our persistent anthropomorphizing of the Others are not difficult to guess. In the end curiosity about the truly strange fades before the ancient wish to be comforted in the vast black night of space. We require that our gods resemble us, else how will they understand our hopes and fears? We must believe that the gods, or the godlike aliens we search for in the night sky, in some sense created us in their image, and to that end, in an act of sympathetic magic, we create them in ours.

This is not to say that in the catalogue of alien forms from science-fiction films there are no totally non-anthropoid creatures. But it can be shown that in all cases the tentacular blobs, the big-brained crustacea and assorted animate slimes are presented in a sense as animals. They are directly related to the bugaboos of horror stories. Inevitably hostile, they invade, like the Martians in *The War of the Worlds*, driven by the most primitive of urges, and no more responsive to an appeal to reason than a marauding column of army ants. It is no wonder that the priest

Ray Harryhausens'
delightfully
animated Cyclops
menaces Sinbad on
his **Seventh Voyage**

INTRODUCTION

who confronts the Martian vehicle in *The War of the Worlds* gets vaporized: as well counsel a hungry crocodile in Platonic moderation.

As animals, the Bug-eyed Monsters are inevitably defeated, either because human cunning prevails over the awesome weaponry of the invading creatures or because of a cosmic accident, such as that which ends *The War of the Worlds*. This fact brings with it the comforting suggestion that there is a power above even the might of the invaders, and that power has human interests at heart.

The paradox attendant on the concept of unreasoning animals equipped with space craft and laser guns can be resolved by looking once again to humankind's origins. *Homo erectus,* peering fearfully from his cave, saw all around him savage beasts whose armament—tooth and claw, speed and strength—was as far superior to his own as the energy beams and force fields of the invading aliens are to contemporary humanity's tanks and machine guns. Thus, the invasion movies' linking of superior weaponry with inferior mentality is simply a modern twist on the archetypal combination of murderous claws and dim wits that stalk our race memories of cave bear and sabre-tooth tiger.

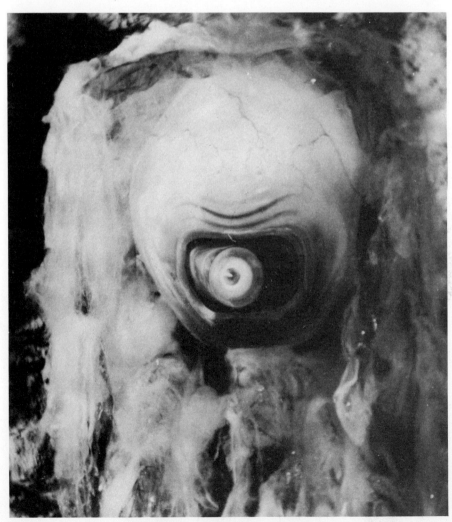

Extremely rare shot of the Xenomorph in its true form.

INTRODUCTION

And just as our ancestors overcame their formidable predators through the exercise of their relatively large brains—humankind's only weapons—so the heroes of the invasion movies continue to memorialize that ancient victory by consistently outsmarting their heavily armed but rather stupid adversaries.

Not without help, however. *2001: A Space Odyssey* suggests that human reason, our ultimate weapon, was itself a gift from humanity's protectors. In the film's opening sequence, ape-men are shown cowering through a night full of menacing teeth and claws . They are helpless and pitiful, no match for their animal adversaries, until the moment when a monolithic teaching device sent to Earth by a godlike alien race stimulates their forebrains into the discovery that a heavy animal femur can be used as a weapon. Thereafter, we are assured, the animal kingdom is delivered into the hairy hands of our forebears. "Somebody up there likes us," indeed. Why? Kubrick and Clarke do not say, but the sequence is a masterful celebration in ritual form of the ancient victory of human reason over brute strength which continues to form the theme of the invasion type of science-fiction film.

Movies featuring animalistic Bug-eyed Monsters can be of high technical quality *(The War of the Worlds)*, and occasionally they manage to make intelligent if pessimistic statements concerning the human condition. *Invasion of the Body Snatchers* concerns itself with a plague of extraterrestrial "pods," which have the power to grow within themselves duplicates of the humans with whom they come in contact. These duplicates, predictably enough, wander around like zombies, gradually taking over the world. The film's director, Don Siegel, had a specific purpose in mind in creating an image of soulless alien simulacra of humanity: "...the world is populated by pods and I wanted to show them." Well and good, but his pods, with the alien bacteria of *The Andromeda Strain* and the rest of the genre of invading non-human creatures, are ultimately tricked-up expressions of the primitive fear of the unknown, which is the theme of the traditional horror story from the cautionary tales of the Brothers Grimm to the giant-insect movies of the 1950s. At their best, the BEM films powerfully evoke the goblins of the human subconscious, one of which, the "Monster from the Id" is the literal villain of *Forbidden Planet,* a film that blends horror tale with hard science fiction—with compelling results. At their worst, in films where technology gone wrong (the Bomb and its attendant radiation, or the machinations of mad scientists) is responsible for the marauding monster, they are expressions of an irrational fear of science, indeed of knowledge itself and the human curiosity that seeks it. These latter films suggest that the medieval preference for superstition over science is still prevalent enough in our times to pay the producers of quickie monster movies handsomely at the box office.

A step up from the ravening Beast from the Stars is the extraterrestrial as galactic human, *homo sapiens* in all but a few cosmetic de-

Facing page:
The Xenomorphs from **It Came from Outer Space** in human guise confront the late Richard Carlson.

A computer scans for signs of **The Andromeda Strain**.

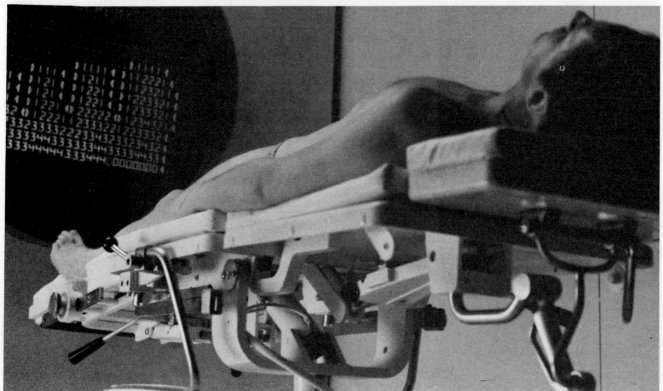

INTRODUCTION

tails. This Star Man has managed, through a process seldom explained, to develop the technology to cross the universe without blowing himself up in the process, and his type figures in by far the greatest number of science-fiction films dealing with extraterrestrials. The serials (direct descendants of the comics and the pulps), for example, pit Homeric heroes such as Buck Rogers and Flash Gordon against malevolent but perfectly human "aliens" whose schemes and ambitions differ only in the patched-on details of rocket ships and bizarre place names from those of earthly tyrants since the invention of politics. Machiavelli would have understood Ming the Merciless quite well, down to the Renaissance cut of his cloak, though he would have found the twenty-fifth-century version of The Prince rather too crude in his methodology to prevail for long (Ming doesn't, of course). The humanoid tyrants command a wide variety of non-human servants, to be sure, and these provide the necessary touch of the exotic without which the serials would be indistinguishable from pirate movies and other swashbuckling costume dramas. But one never finds a non-human creature in overall command, and the message of the serials, insofar as there is one outside the bully-boy notion that the square-jawed will prevail, seems to be that "out there" we'll find people just like us, only meaner.

Moving outside the comic-strip derring-do of the serials, we continue to find the humanoid alien a dominant figure in feature films. He is not always evil, of course: we have mentioned Klaatu in *The Day the Earth Stood Still*, who comes in peace but with a warning, like a sort of cosmic conscience. Spock, the "Vulcan" in the *"Star Trek"* TV series works along with Earthlings on board the Star Ship *Enterprise*, tempering the humans' insatiable curiosity and unruly passions with his cool rationality—his only really "alien" quality, (beyond his pointed ears)—a philosophical ideal long sought on Earth, but never achieved.

The humanoid alien is accessible. He represents us either as we fear or wish to be. It is comforting to imagine that the invention of a faster-than-light drive or a teleport beam will not produce essential changes in the human species; doubly so to think that cultures that may have already developed such devices look and feel and behave as we do. It is a truism to say that we fear the consequences of our own runaway technology, and the science-fiction film's preoccupation with humanoid aliens—benevolent older brothers who have already surmounted the social and psychological difficulties technology brings with it—reflects our common desire for reassurance that our present problems are eventually solvable.

In films that treat extraterrestrials as benevolent, the deistic conclusion is almost inescapable. The advanced technology of the visitors becomes the divine might of the gods, and their self-revelation produces upon humanity an effect comparable to the experience of the mystic who sees his deity face to face. God as alien astronaut is variously handled. In *The Man Who Fell to Earth*, David Bowie's accidental visitor is seen as a Christ figure. Similarly, Klaatu in *The Day the Earth Stood*

Babies dangle from trees in this early pulp illustration by J. Allen St. John.

Facing page:
Gort breaks into jail to retrieve the lifeless body of Klaatu.

INTRODUCTION

Still, the "human" emissary of an all-powerful race watching over humankind, recapitulates the events of the Passion: He is wounded and eventually killed, but he is resurrected in time to deliver his message.

The venerable Ben Kenobe, prophet figure of *Star Wars,* is a member of a mystic martial order that derives directly from the Knights Templars and Hospitallers of the crusades, and in chivalric piety he sacrifices himself deliberately in order to pass "The Force"—a somewhat sketchy version of the Demiurge that animates the universe—to a younger disciple.

These alien Christs and prophets, whose human forms restate the anthropomorphism of the Judaeo-Christian tradition (God is just like you and me, only better), reflect the unwillingness of most science-fiction film makers to venture outside popular prejudices concerning the nature of humanity's relationship to the cosmos. We do not like to think that God—or an alien race so far removed from our limitations as to seem godlike—may not be motivated by any of our primary concerns. We prefer Him (or Her or It) in a presentable human envelope. But we thereby deny God His Godhood—the limitless freedom of choice that a mature theology ascribes to Him as a first principle. Science-fiction film, as technology's version of theological speculation, persists in the same delusion—with some important exceptions that suggest that the field is approaching the degree of courageous sophistication science-fiction literature attained as long ago as the late 1930s, when Olaf Stapledon spun his metaphysical fantasy of the search for the Star Maker.

In *It Came from Outer Space* (whose original screen treatment was done by Ray Bradbury, a master of science-fiction writing) the aliens themselves are never seen. Instead, they take over the bodies of various Earthlings—but the "invasion" is not sinister, in the horror-movie sense of *Invasion of the Body Snatchers.* The alien spacecraft, beautifully realized as a glowing prismatic shape that eludes mechanistic classification, has suffered a breakdown, and the aliens are simply borrowing the bodies of human beings so that they can obtain the necessary spare parts. Once repaired, the ship proceeds toward its unguessable destination. Although the breakdown suggests an ineptitude on the aliens' part hardly evocative of godly omnipotence, the fact that the aliens are here by accident, are not at all concerned with the doings of humanity, and depart without explanations suggest that Jack Arnold, the film's director, was exploring the possibility that a culture advanced enough to have developed star travel may simply not be interested in the naked, Earthbound ape. In other words, if God is an astronaut, it is rank human chauvinism to suppose that we are anything but a minor incident in a mission whose aims we cannot imagine.

2001: A Space Odyssey—to which another of the most important science-fiction writers, Arthur C. Clarke, was a principle contributor—tackles the problem head on. All our versions of God, according to the film, are simply attempts to remember the alien mentors who have guided human development. Clarke's fiction is a blend of understated

mysticism and meticulously researched technology. He has concerned himself, from the seminal *Childhood's End* to his recent *Rendezvous with Rama,* with undermining anthropocentrism by presenting cases in which first contact with aliens forces us to realize not only that we are not alone in the universe, but also that we are far from being the first concern of those who are its masters. Kubrick's film adaptation of Clarke's proposition is equally provocative. Rejecting his original decision to show the alien builders of the monoliths, he leaves them as ambiguous as any concept of a god beyond human understanding must be. His final image—the astronaut reborn as star child gazing down on the Earth with innocent, wise eyes—suggests that only when we have cast off our notion of ourselves as the center of creation will we be privileged to walk and talk with the gods.

Finally, *Close Encounters of the Third Kind* presents the moment in which the extraterrestrial gods reveal themselves directly. Spielberg draws more upon the "factual" lore of UFO sightings than upon the images of science-fiction films: His jewel-like spacecraft are ultimately flying saucers, and his aliens are the two types that have most frequently cropped up in the annals of UFOlogy. It can be argued that in deciding to strip the gods of their mystery by showing them on the screen, Spielberg's version of the meeting of human beings with the lords of creation is less provocative than that of Kubrick and Clarke. But even granted the limitations Spielberg imposed upon himself by adhering to the dictates of UFOlogy, the film surrounds its aliens with enough of the paradoxical, not to say mystical, to achieve a convincing vision of the possible nature of beings whose essence is beyond human comprehension. Although the film's special effects are breathtaking, Spielberg wisely chose to concentrate upon the various human reactions to the coming of the aliens, a visit attended by impossible phenomena according to conventional wisdom. Human anthropocentrism is the target, and from the unconscious presumption of the scientist who asks, "Are we the first?" of a Mexican *federale* already at the site where a squadron of World War II aircraft have mysteriously appeared, to the moment when the gigantic mother ship of the aliens touches down amid

INTRODUCTION

a circle of dazed human technicians, we are witness to Spielberg's efforts at consciousness-raising. How successful he is depends of course upon his audience's hardheadedness (the film is not without flaws). But it stands, with *2001: A Space Odyssey,* as the most ambitious effort to date to present the total Otherness that both science and religion have long maintained to be a necessary attribute of godlike beings.

The film is also a celebration of technology on a grand scale—both the technology of the aliens and of the cinema itself. As such it is something of a rarity among science-fiction movies, the majority of which exhibit a strongly anti-science bias along with a racism rooted in xenophobia. The spirit lying beneath the swashbuckling and the implausible cardboard monsters of the pulp-derived '30s and '40s serials and the Z-grade movies of the '50s blatantly reflects popular American attitudes at the times the films were made. Isolationist racism peeps from the shadows of Buck Rogers' and Flash Gordon's toylike Deco spaceships: Significantly, both heroes were doing battle with villains whose "alienness' consisted solely in their Oriental features. And although the Buck Rogers serial does not go as far in the direction of Yellow Peril paranoia as the original comic strip in the 1920s (which is set on a twentyfifth-century Earth where "Mongols" have conquered everyone but a tiny handful of intrepid WASPs), it does set a trend in science-fiction films that has continued unbroken until quite recently.

The xenophobia of the horror movie was ideally suited to the murky atmosphere of suspicion and betrayal that nearly choked Hollywood during the McCarthy years, and science-fiction invasion movies from those times imply, consciously or not, that outside the rigid boundaries of "traditional" American values everyone and everything is to be feared, hated, hunted down and destroyed. In 1954, as the junior Senator from Wisconsin was nearing the end of his paranoid career, still ful-

The Burroughs-like Bantha roams the sands of Tatooine in George Lucas' epic space fantasy, **Star Wars**.

INTRODUCTION

minating against the godless Communists and their ghostly manipulations of American hearts and minds, William Cameron Menzies produced a 3-D film whose theme of mental manipulation could have been borrowed directly from McCarthy's fantasies. In his *Invaders from Mars* a loathsome Martian mastermind (represented Oz-wise by a disembodied head), surrounded by brainwashed mutants, landed on Earth and by emplanting mysterious crystals in the brains of Earthlings, attempted to repopulate the planet with docile slaves. The aliens' plan was foiled by a combination of courageous innocence and good old American military know-how: A young boy managed to convince the Army of the reality of the menace, and the bodiless brain was blown away. Menzies, whose 1936 adaptation of H. G. Wells' *The Shape of Things to Come* had taken an interesting, if inconsistent, look at the consequences of jingoism and rampant nationalism, relapsed into knee-jerk conservatism with *Invaders from Mars*. It is regrettable that the high imagination that characterized many of the film's special effects and background sequences did not carry over into the handling of the subject matter.

The Martian mastermind from William Cameron Menzies' **Invaders from Mars**.

Nor are contemporary science-fiction film makers immune to charges of creeping xenophobia and racism. Perhaps too much fuss has been made about *Star Wars's* lily-white cast of Aryan heroes. George Lucas has insisted that he was simply trying to add sophisticated special effects to the traditional swashbuckling space opera, and symbol-seeking rather spoils the fun. Nevertheless, because of the nature of Lucas's pulp and serial sources, the social attitude of *Star Wars* is a blend of gee-whiz weaponry worship and rampant "Americanism," which any Buck Rogers fan can recognize. As a presentation of a possible future society (the lead-in phrase "Long ago, in a distant galaxy…" is an artful dodge), the film can be misleading, especially to children, its major audience. In a recent edition of *The Village Voice* a young black street kid, taken to the movie by a *Voice* reporter, emerges asking, "Is that all true? Where are all the black people?" They're there, all right, though only arch-villain Darth Vader, whose ominous voice beneath the ebony mask belongs to James Earl Jones, is black. They come in green, hairy-brown and parti-color. Only one of the whole non-Aryan bunch of them is friendly, and he, the Wookiee Chewbacca is a sort of idiot-savant, a shambling bearlike being who has somehow been taught astrogation, but whose relationship to his pilot (white, of course) is more that of dangerous pet to master than of man to man.

More obvious than creeping racism, the anti-science attitude of the majority of science-fiction films similarly reflects the social fears of popular culture. This thread ties in with the older phobias of the horror movie, discussed above in treating the Frankenstein motif: Man should not tamper with nature's processes. The real villains in *The War of the Worlds,* for example, are not the invading Martians themselves, who are glimpsed only briefly and appear as relatively frail creatures. Rather, the terrifying Martian machines provide the film's menace—the grace-

INTRODUCTION

ful deadly cobra-headed attack vehicles that float around impersonally murdering everyone according to no human rationale. The film, released in 1953 during the gathering popular reaction against what was seen as a soulless technology that had placed all humanity under the shadow of the Bomb, accurately portrays the sullen helplessness infecting the country at the time. It implies that as science continues to advance it will increasingly limit its activities to the development of weaponry. The ultimate manipulators of that weaponry, their humanity contaminated in the name of science, emerge as blindly malevolent power seekers. Their film presentation as "Martians"—at a time when "alien" Chinese and North Koreans were battling Americans in the skies over Korea and even more frighteningly faceless technicians on both sides of the Iron Curtain were assumed to be preparing nuclear Doomsday Machines for Armageddon—is simply a question of cosmetics.

Mistrust of technology, inspired most immediately by fear of the Bomb, finds subtler roots in the threat to personal identity posed by a

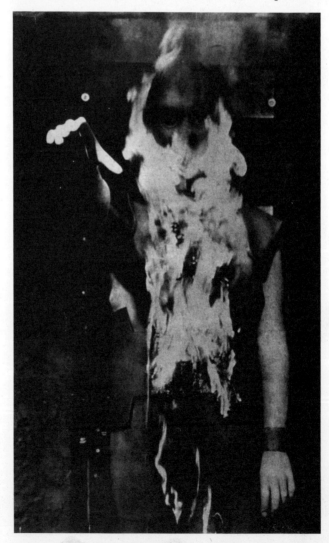

An apocalyptic vision of tomorrow as an android burns from Ib Melchior's **The Time Travellers**.

Commander Adams forces Morbius to confront his alter ego, the Id monster in the thrilling climax of **Forbidden Planet**.

society increasingly dominated by the imperatives of the machine. Popular sociological studies of the 1950s, such as *The Man in the Gray Flannel Suit,* depict a world in which conformity is the rule and the computerized production schedule is king. The "pod people" of *Invasion of the Body Snatchers,* as we have seen, are intended to reflect the director's view of a faceless corporate society populated by human robots.

Moving into the 1960s we find the anti-technology bias still flourishing in such films as Losey's *These Are the Damned,* Truffaut's *Fahrenheit 451* and Godard's *Alphaville.* Although none of these films deal with aliens, they should be mentioned as more or less traditional warnings, along the lines of *Things to Come,* about the consequences of the continued worship of technology for technology's sake. The theme seems ingrained, and the sudden emergence of *2001: A Space Odyssey* in opposition to it comes as a welcome relief. The only major film of the '60s that concerned itself with aliens, *2001* also presents for the first time a future in which humanity has come to comfortable terms with technology. The film's visual hymns to the majesty of space travel stress the obvious but seldom-stated fact that what seems mind-boggling to us will be routine to the next generation: the vast wheel of the space station rolls around its orbit to the *gemütlich* strains of "The Blue Danube Waltz." Kubrick's and Clarke's depiction of technology is not an unqualified rave, of course. The humans who move with such ease through

INTRODUCTION

space-station corridors are all rather sterile, and the immaculate plastic interiors suggest that the decor of the near future will be primarily Motel Modern. But if human technology, in the film, is still seen as dehumanizing, technology, in the form of the super-science of the alien mentors, provides the solution to the problem.

This point needs clarification. In a sense, the most human character of *2001* is a machine; the computer HAL 9000. The nominally human cast operates within such a narrow emotional range that it is inconceivable that any of them could suffer anything so violent as a nervous breakdown. But HAL does, and sets out methodically to destroy his human masters. On the one hand HAL can be seen as a traditional image of technology gone wild. But in the moving sequence in which the surviving astronaut "kills" him, HAL ironically serves as a figure for the human mind itself—the astronaut who goes about the murder emotionlessly emerging as the machine that destroys it.

But the image, like most images in the film, is deliberately ambiguous. Once HAL has been shut down the ship is without control, and the astronaut, bereft of the benefits of human technology, must fall back on the bare fact of his humanity as his derelict craft continues on its preordained journey to rendezvous with the alien mentors of mankind. And the technology of these beings, brilliantly evoked by Kubrick through an exploitation of the total resources of film technology itself, is far beyond the depersonalizing hardware of twentyfirst-century Earth. It is, indeed, technology raised into mysticism, as much pure mind as machine. In depicting, through a dazzling series of visual images, the experience of the astronaut as he passes through what is at once a physical journey and an initiation rite, Kubrick aligns himself firmly with those physicists who operate along the leading edge of their science. There Western determinism meets Eastern god-consciousness in the noumenal haze of quantum mechanics, relativity and the uncertainty principle of Heisenberg: Nothing can be "known," in the mechanical sense, and science must rely on intuition. The next step in science will involve what we can only call mysticism. *2001's* aliens have already made it, and their message to humanity is that we have already reached the limits of mechanistic technology. Further expansion of our knowledge of the nature of phenomena will require a quantum jump in consciousness: at last, with the star child we will be fully at home in the cosmos, and the line between technology and the workings of the spirit will dissolve.

And I looked, and, behold, a whirlwind came out of the north, a great cloud, and a fire infolding itself, and a brightness was about it, and out of the midst thereof as the color of amber, out of the midst of the fire. Also out of the midst thereof came the likeness of four living creatures. And this was their appearance: they had the likeness of a man.

—Ezekiel, I, iv-vi

Cosmologists like Carl Sagan have suggested that although the odds

Facing page:
When Russian cosmonauts landed on Mars, they discovered the strange civilization of **Aelita**.

INTRODUCTION

for the existence of rational life elsewhere in the galaxy are good, the odds that it will have evolved according to the human model are miniscule. Our bodies, to say nothing of our minds, are but one of many possible responses life can offer to a given set of environmental conditions. Beings evolving, say, on a planet of a star that radiates more strongly in the ultraviolet end of the spectrum than does our sun, will have very different ideas about color than we do, and the effects of this single difference upon their intellectual development will be large indeed. Add to the differences in form and attitude resulting from a nonterrestrial planetary environment (those contingent on the emotional maturity which beings capable of developing a truly integrated technology must logically possess), and the picture becomes strange indeed, in human terms. In a recent *Playboy* interview J. Allen Hynek, a longtime UFO researcher and professor of astronomy who was a technical consultant for Spielberg's *Close Encounters of the Third Kind,* sums up the issue: "...if we were visited by another race from a distant planet, it is unlikely that they would be humanoid in shape and even more unlikely that one could read their emotions." He suggests further in the discussion, "Let's not be anthropomorphic.... Their motivations don't have to fit our ideas. As any contact with them will be solely at their discretion, all we can do is speculate." In other words, it is rather doubtful that an alien culture would take the trouble to visit our planetary outback for any human reason. The greatest weakness of the science-fiction film until recently has been its simpleminded insistence on presenting aliens as humans in weird drag: Pulp-derived images of monsters from the stars (or the collective unconscious) dragging off our women (one wonders what they can do with the poor ladies, besides devour them) or blowing up our cities tell far more about the human film makers and their audience than they do about the aliens, as we have seen.

Close Encounters of the Third Kind, like *2001* before it, does much to repair the science-fiction film's reputation for naïveté in the matter of extraterrestrial visitation. At first glance we are on familiar ground here. We recognize the paranoid military machine that attempts to deal with the inexplicable by covering it up. The Air Force major, who alternately waffles and threatens when he is asked for answers by ordinary citizens who have had close encounters, would be at home in any of the monster invasion films of the 1950s, though the sinister aspects of the cover-up are a product of our post-Watergate era.

Our old friend the benign but misguided superscientist is here as well, played by François Truffaut, whose 1966 *Fahrenheit 451* presented an attitude toward the "plasticalization" of human values similar to the one displayed by Spielberg in this film. Functioning within the system, even his pure desire for knowledge cannot prevent him from collusion with the petty military tyrants.

But after these, all similarities to the typical human characters of alien-encounter films ceases. The film's nominal hero, Richard Drey-

François Truffaut, director of **Fahrenheit 451** portrays Claude Lacombe, the leader of an international UFO investigating team in **Close Encounters of the Third Kind**.

Rotwang, the
scientist, shows off
his latest creation—
Maria the Robot—to
John Masterman,
leader of Fritz Lang's
Metropolis.

INTRODUCTION

fuss, is no square-jawed meathead out to "stop the alien menace." He is an ordinary man faced with an utterly extraordinary phenomenon, and the film, concentrating on his frantic search for an answer—which results in the loss of his job, his friends and his family—follows him through a journey as spiritual as it is physical. Finally, stripped of the conventional trappings of middle America and its conventional mental habits as well, he is accepted into communion with the aliens, having achieved the all-accepting sense of humble wonder, which was his birthright as a child.

The child himself, a four-year-old who reacts to the incredible lights and sounds of the alien ships with delighted glee, is perhaps the real hero of the film. His sense of wonder, set against the panic and paranoia of the adults, recalls Christ's message to His disciples: In order to enter the Kingdom of Heaven you must become as little children. Divine—or truly alien—mysteries cannot be anatomized, but only accepted with profound humility and gratitude.

The aliens of the film, like the gods, are selective in their summons to humanity. Minds bogged down in prejudices and materialism cannot "hear" the summons, and must undergo further purification before they will be eligible for existence on the aliens' plane of understanding. That plane is represented by the extraordinary special effects of the film. The aliens are presented in terms of pure light and sound. Their ships seem to slide from corporeality to insubstantiality as easily as they perform "impossible" maneuvers in the sky—maneuvers that are purposeful, to be sure, but wonderfully playful as well. Indeed, play is an important element in the film. The little boy refers to the lights in the sky as "toys," and the aliens take an impish delight in making his toys and the clumsier "toys" of his mother's kitchen assume a life of their own. Oven doors slam open and shut, windup tanks reel about drunkenly, refrigerators spit their plastic contents all over the room. The message is obvious: Put away your childish things, your gadgets and parlor tricks. Grow up. One of the bureaucratic scientists, shocked into a re-evaluation of human presumption when the aliens begin to unfold their real powers, remarks to a colleague that it's the first day of school.

The religious implications of the film are made still clearer in the breathtaking sequence in which the mother ship of the aliens touches down. It is a cathedral of light and it "speaks" a musical language in the voice of a thousand organ pipes, majestic and terrifying. The choice of music as the communications medium between the alien emissaries and the Earthlings is inspired. On the one hand, the principles of music, mathematical and precise, are universal enough to be understood by cultures as vastly different as ours and an immensely evolved alien society. And on the other, music expresses all that is at once abstractly pure and profoundly sensual in the human spirit. It is the appropriate language of the gods, and the proper companion to the film's use of light, which celebrates the marriage of matter and energy at the heart of both physics and religion.

Exeter, and his crew
explains to the
Earthians the
reasons for their
abduction
(from **This Island Earth**)

INTRODUCTION

Close Encounters of the Third Kind, with *2001: A Space Odyssey*, is the finest evocation to date, in the science-fiction film, of a plausible alien race. The years since Méliès' crustacean Sélénites have seen the most remote of Shakespeare's "Antres vast and desarts idle" thoroughly mapped, and their most peculiar denizens reduced to unwilling subjects for sociological dissertations. We have also gone from the last gasp of the Age of Sail to the first bellowings of the Rocket Age, and we now travel to the Moon in less time than it took Méliès and his contemporaries to cross the Atlantic. Our search for the remote and fabulous can take place only in space, and the possibility of advanced alien civilizations somewhere Out There has changed from a bizarre speculation to a near certinty. Mr. Hynek, in the *Playboy* interview quoted above, compares us, in our little system at the tip of a wide-flung arm of the Milky Way, to "...natives of a remote region of the Yukon who are totally unaware of the intricate civilization far to the south..." Or rather, to extend the image, we Yukonites have just begun to hear rumors about our awesome neighbors, and in films like *Close Encounters of the Third Kind* we are finally beginning to speculate intelligently about their possible nature.

The science-fiction film's picture of alien beings has changed to fit our growing sophistication about our position in the cosmos. Monster movies and space operas will of course continue to be made, as the success of Lucas's *Star Wars* attests. But as we come to grips with the problems—and accept, on a warier and more intelligent level the benefits—of technology, we will be better equipped to extrapolate from the state of our own science to the capabilities of a star-traveling culture. Understanding that high technology deeply affects the world view and psychology of its exploiters and victims—that craft and spirit are inevitably linked—will condition us for the moment of first contact with a higher civilization. Perhaps it is an error to predict that the alien will come in friendship. We do not fully understand our own natures, and it is hubristic to speculate concerning the nature of a totally different sentient race before we have answered our own questions. But the error is certainly no worse than its converse; to predict that the aliens will attack us like so many Monsters from the Id, using their godlike powers only to imitate a pack of human looters on a spree in a blackout. The point is moot, but personally I prefer the qualified optimism of films like *2001* and *Close Encounters*. In a time of widespread confusion, hatred and despair, these films provide vital food for the spirit by suggesting that life indeed evolves from a lower to a higher state, that entropy can in some way be resisted, and that we are not alone.

—B. Tompkins

Four-year-old Cary Guffey reaches for the EXTIs as Melinda Dillon supresses her terror.

Flash Gordon battles a hybrid of Mars. (Painting by Gogos and Warren).

Teenagers and townspeople rush to Steve McQueen's aid in **The Blob.**

42 (Cont.)

                              KLAATU
                   We have come to visit you in peace --
                   and with good will.

       Klaatu walks slowly down the ramp toward the soldiers.
       As he does so, he draws from inside his tunic a strange-
       looking object, longish and tubular. It might be a
       telescope -- or it might be some strange kind of weapon.

43   MED. SHOT

       shooting from the side, showing Klaatu advancing slowly
       toward the line of soldiers. He holds out the mysterious
       object in front of him in a gesture that is actually one
       of offering but could be misinterpreted as menacing.
       There is a growing, uneasy rumble of muttering among the
       soldiers as Klaatu advances. They are clearly frightened
       of what he may do.

44   CLOSE SHOT - PLATOON LEADER

       A young second lieutenant, standing in front of his
       platoon. As Klaatu advances, the lieutenant unslings
       his carbine.

45   MED. SHOT

       Klaatu starts toward the platoon leader, raising the
       object he holds toward the man, trying to make clear his
       intentions. Misinterpreting this as a menacing gesture,
       the platoon leader raises his carbine to his shoulder.

46   MED. CLOSE SHOT

       of one of the tank commanders in the turret of his tank.
       He is watching Klaatu advancing toward the platoon leader
       and he has drawn his pistol. Convinced that the lieuten-
       ant is in jeopardy, the tank commander aims at Klaatu and
       fires.

47   MED. SHOT

       as Klaatu falls to the ground wounded. The object he was
       holding has dropped from his hand and smashed. The sol-
       diers start to gather around Klaatu excitedly when sud-
       denly there appears in the entrance to the space ship a
       huge robot. There is a gasp of amazement from the crowd
       and the soldiers draw back at sight of him. The robot is
       ten feet tall, is made in the almost-perfect image of a
       man. He is to be played by an actor and his flesh appears
       to be made of a greenish metal. His eyes flash as though
       lighted internally. His perfectly-fashioned, muscular
       body is covered only with a loincloth. This is GORT.
       There are cries of amazement as Gort walks slowly, pon-
       derously, down the ramp to the ground. As he does so,

                                               (CONTINUED)

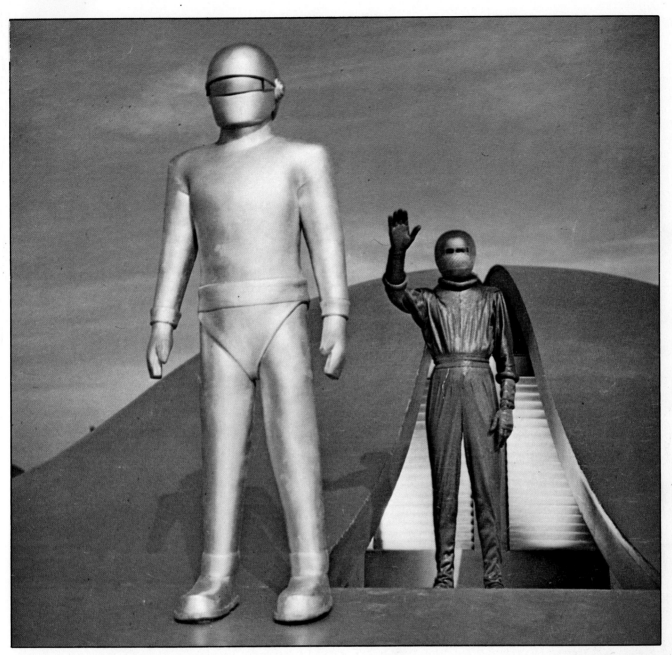

Klaatu and Gort have
arrived on Earth. From
**The Day The Earth Stood
Still.**

The original, shooting
script from Robert Wise's
classic **The Day The Earth
Stood Still.**

The French poster for
This Island Earth.

A peaceful first encounter with a race of Wally Wood beauties from **Wierd Science** #14. Copyright © 1978, by William M. Gaines.

The Healer as illustrated by Emsh for **Astounding** magazine.

August 1956 · 35 Cents

Astounding
SCIENCE FICTION.

The
Healer

Jimmy Hunt and Helena Carter at the mercy of the **Invaders from Mars.**

The alien-controlled parents from **Invaders from Mars** attempt to reclaim "their" son.

The Martian council
tries to discredit
Yuri, the cosmonaut,
in **Aelita**.

CHAPTER ONE

FLASH GORDON AND DESCENDANTS

Created in 1934 by the illustrious Alex Raymond, Flash Gordon began his exploits on the four-color pages of the Sunday funnies. Flash, the intrepid Dr. Alexi Zharkov, and the always imperiled Dale Arden rocketed into the void of space when Earth was faced with annihilation from the onrushing planetoid Mongo.

Mongo was, however—inhabited by the most bizarre grotesqueries that lurked in the recesses of Raymond's dark dreams. Hawkmen, Lionmen, Sharkmen, Menmen, aquatic Octosacs, dragons of Tao, horned orangopods all did their part to make Flash's stay on Mongo quite unpleasant

Princess Aura, the daughter of the self-proclaimed Emperor of the Universe, Ming the Merciless, was quite pleasant, however. Not only did Raymond draw the best rayguns, rocketships, and alien creatures, he drew the sexiest women.

In 1936 Buster Crabbe realized Flash in the most expensive movie serial ever made. *Flash Gordon* set the standard, and others followed. *Buck Rogers* (played also by the durable Crabbe) exploded in a twelve-chapter serial. Then Flash took a *Trip To Mars* and shortly thereafter *Conquered the Universe*. Later, *Superman* from the planet Krypton soared in live action and animation onto the silver screen.

Facing page:
The King of the Clay people, Flash, and Prince Barin— rightful ruler of Mongo—plot against the evil queen of Mars (from **Flash Gordon's Trip to Mars**).

Dr. Zharkov (Frank Shannon), Flash Gordon (Buster Crabbe), and Dale are captured by the minions of Ming the Merciless upon their arrival on the Planet Mongo from the 1936 Universal serial **Flash Gordon** based on the classic comic strip by Alex Raymond.

Overleaf:
The Zuggs of Saturn aid in the capture of one of the Earthmen (from the Universal serial **Buck Rogers**).

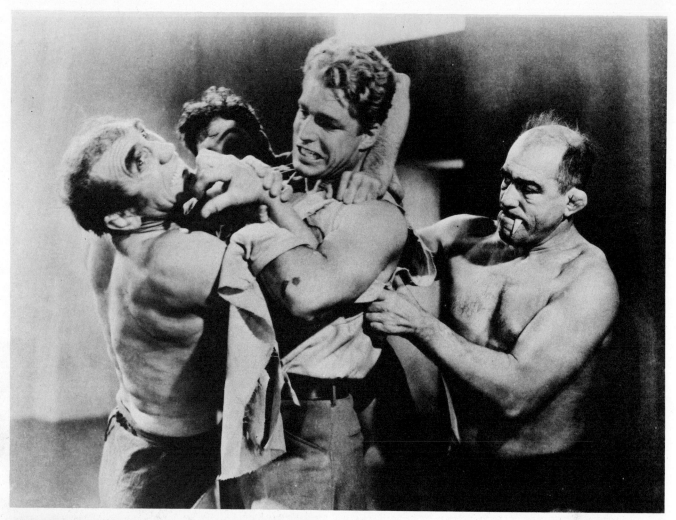

Flash and company are seized by King Vultan's Hawkmen and taken to his city in the sky.

Flash does battle with the Savages of Mongo in the **Arena of Death**.

Ming the Merciless, self-proclaimed Ruler of the Universe (Charles Middleton), signals an underling.

Buck (Buster Crabbe), Dr. Huer, and Wilma Deering explain to Prince Talon of Saturn (Phillip Ahn) why the Saturnians should support the rebel forces.

Flash faces death, again, at the hands of a malevolent Martian.

Buck leads a
Saturnian
commando raid
against Killer Kane's
men.

The Rock people of
Mongo (in their
protective armor)
attempt to carry off
Dale (Carol Hughes)
while Flash protests
(from **Flash Gordon
Conquers the
Universe** 1940).

Facing page:
Republic pictures classic **Zombies of the Stratosphere** featured Martian gangsters and a pre–**Star Trek** Leonard Nimoy.

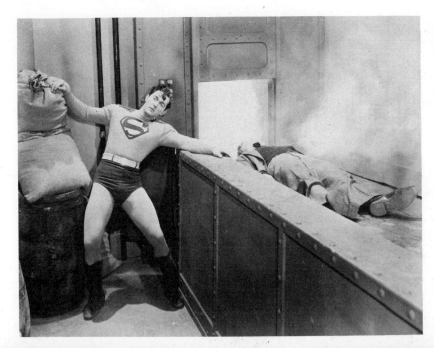

Superman (Kirk Alyn) is overcome by a substance, Kryptonite, from his home world, Krypton.

Superman from the planet Krypton, demonstrates his heat vision from a Max Fleischer **Superman** cartoon.

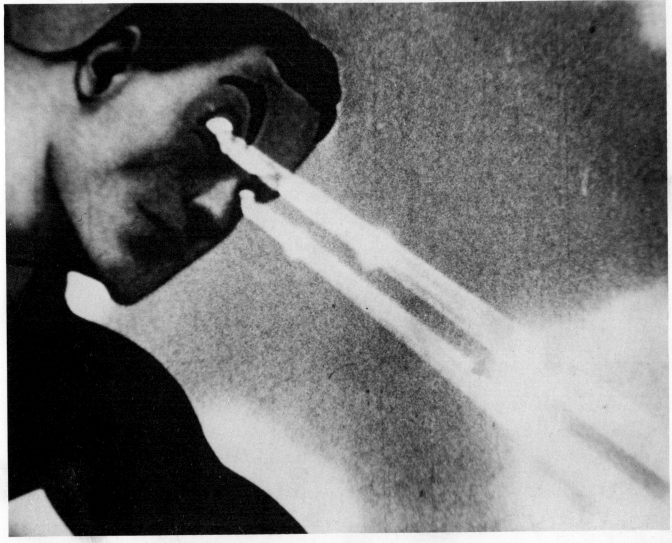

A scene from the
1953 Columbia
serial, **The Lost
Planet** with Judd
Holdren.

Chewbacca, the Wookiee and Han Solo attempt to escape from the Death Star. (Note: crossbow not included in film)

Right:
Barbarella and Tigar are at the mercy of the maleficent Black Queen.

An amplification of Emperor Wang's personage spoofs Harryhausen's Cyclops (from **Flesh Gordon**)

Luke Skywalker (Mark Hamill) and his landspeeder on his home planet, Tatooine.

Preproduction painting by Ralph McQuarrie depicting the Cantina sequence.

Princess Leia (Carrie Fisher) queries, "You talking to me?" as she prepares to defend herself aboard her Rebel Blockade Runner.

CHAPTER TWO

INVASION EARTH: 1950 A.D.

In 1947 a businessman flying over Mt. Rainier in Washington spotted one and coined the term "flying saucer." Three years later, in the frozen wasteland of the Arctic, a flying saucer bearing *The Thing From Another World* crashed, and the invasion of Earth began.

The Thing was an intelligent carrot with vampiric tendencies that had no desire for peaceful coexistence with Earthians. It was promptly electrocuted.

But still they invaded—to capture our scientific geniuses (*This Island Earth*), our women (*The Mysterians*), our teenagers (*Invasion of the Saucermen*), our parents (*Invaders From Mars*), and our souls (*Invasion of the Body Snatchers*).

Rarely did they *not* want *something* of us: Stop your explorations into space (*Earth Vs. the Flying Saucers*); stop your atomic testing (*The Day the Earth Stood Still*); stop your contamination of the universe, were the ultimatums. Only the Xenomorphs from *It Came From Outer Space* wanted time—time to repair their disabled starship and leave this backward sphere. Ray Harryhausen's Ymir traveled *Twenty Million Miles to Earth* accidentally, only to meet an untimely demise atop the Colosseum in Rome.

As the world smoldered at the hands of the merciless extraterrestrials, scientists and military labored around the clock in the attempt to give mankind a reprieve. Invariably Hugh Marlowe or Richard Carlson would conceive the *Deus Ex Machina* (e.g. anti-saucer ray) that would save mankind.

Even God lent a hand and felled the Martian invaders of *War of the Worlds* with His swift bacterial sword.

Facing page:
The disabled prismatic ship from **It Came from Outer Space** with Richard Carlson in the foreground.

Kenneth Tobey and his men approximate the size of the downed saucer in the arctic

Top right:

James Arness (in his pre-**Gunsmoke** days), as "The Thing," lies immobilized in a block of ice.

Bottom right:

Grown from cells of the extraterrestrial plantlike "Thing," are these little "things" who thrive on human blood.

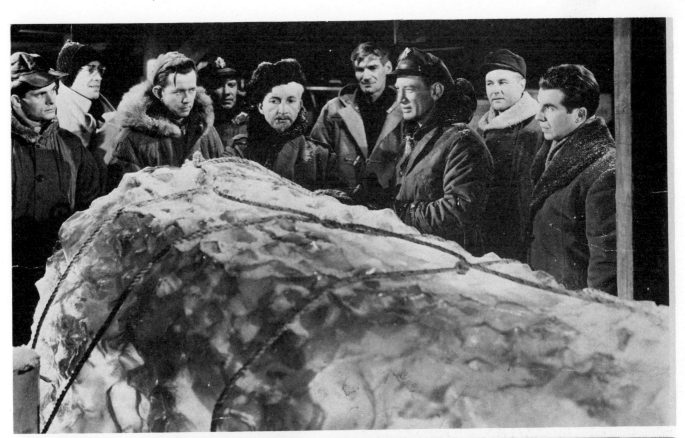

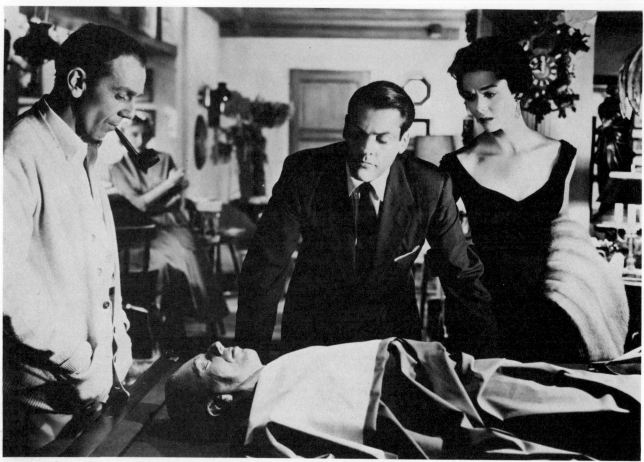

Upon his return to their hiding place, McCarthy kisses Wynter only to discover that now she too, is an emotionless pod.

King Donovan, Kevin McCarthy, and Dana Wynter stare in disbelief at the "blank" in Donovan's home (from **Invasion of the Body Snatchers**).

Right:

"How to Make a Movie Poster, #1"— Gort menaces Patricia Neal in **The Day the Earth Stood Still.**

Top right:

The finished poster gives the false impression of another "Invasion" film.

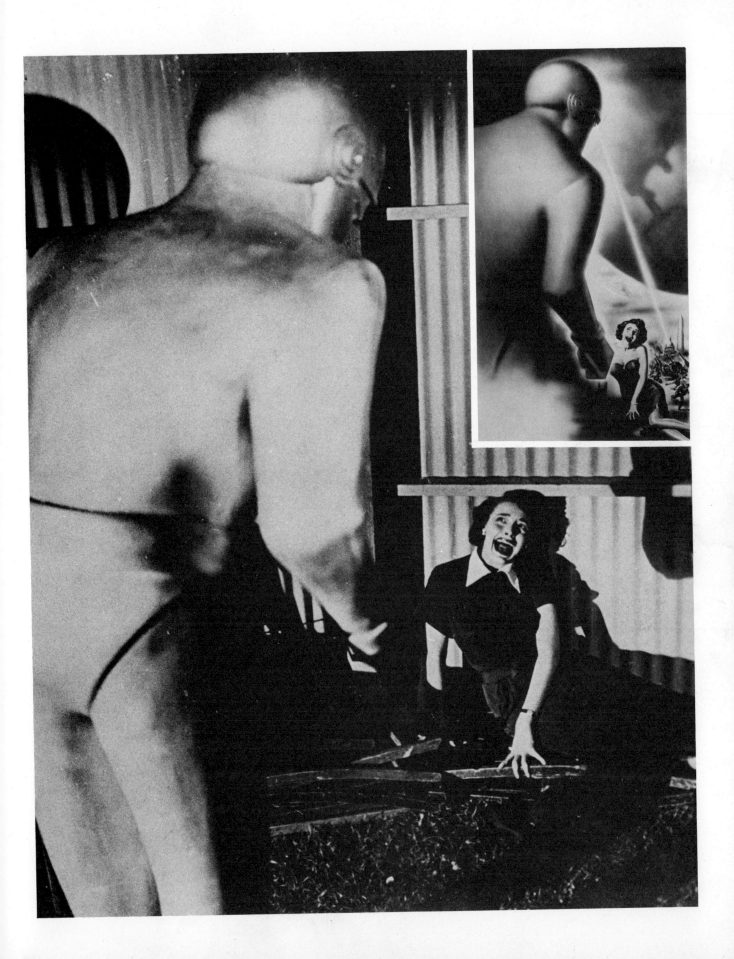

Val guest's **Enemy from Outer Space** speculates what could happen if a human fell into a vat of alien chemicals.

The Metalunans prepare to capture Rex Reason (from **This Island Earth**).

INVASION EARTH: 1950 A.D.

The Hydrocephalonic horrors from the Planet Mars face death at the hands of irresponsible teenagers and their car headlights (from the **Invasion of the Saucermen**).

Tom Tryon portrays the extraterrestrial spouse in **I Married a Monster from Outer Space**.

iumiummiumiumiumiumiumiumiumiumumiumiumum

Washington's most treasured landmarks are levelled by the invading forces in **Earth vs. the Flying Saucers.**

Malevolent Martian machinery on the march, from George Pal's classic **War of the Worlds**.

A martian juggernaut from H. G. Welles' **War of the Worlds**.

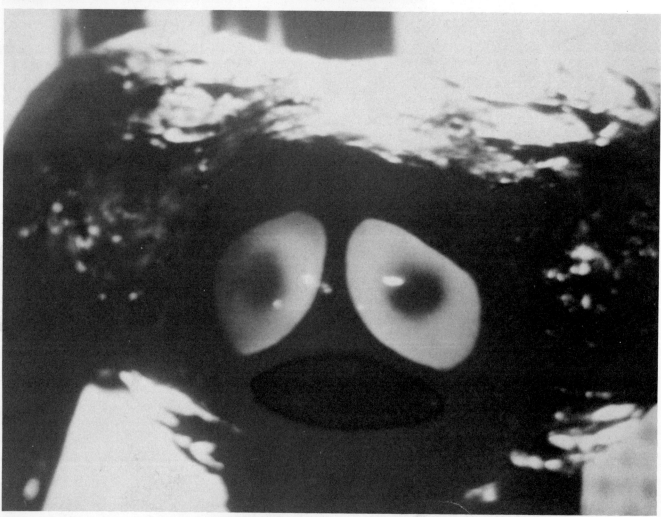

Overleaf:
"And God in His most infinite wisdom…"—The death of the Martians caused by Earthian bacteria.

CHAPTER THREE
LOW-BUDGET INVADERS

After the initial success of the studio-made science-fiction films of the early fifties, small producers jumped on the alien-exploitation bandwagon. Usually shot in a few days on a low budget, their films featured cardboard sets, cardboard actors, and cardboard creatures. It may be noted, however, that in some instances the lower the budget, the more outlandish the aliens.

On the moon were discovered unsavory rock creatures and beautiful women, when the stereotypical scientist and his assistants (including his lovely niece and a punk from Brooklyn) took a *Missile To the Moon*. On the planet Nova was the obligatory stock footage from *One Million B.C.* of Gila monsters masquerading as *King Dinosaur*. Space travel was never so economical as when our intrepid "rocketmen" encountered *Fire Maidens of Outer Space*.

Invaders abounded in all shapes and sizes. Cucumbers (*It Conquered the World*), disemboided brains (*The Brain From Planet Arous*), crabs (*Attack of the Crab Monsters*), Teenagers (*From Outer Space*), and slime (*The Green Slime*) were all jumbled in viewers' minds. Atomic radiation, space travel, blobs, and misguided scientists all got the blame for these travesties of SF.

In the sixties the tradition of "low-bud" hierarchy continued. Santa Claus went to Mars and brought Christendom's most cherished celebration to the planet's wayward inhabitants (*Santa Claus Conquers the Martians*). *Ghidrah the Threeheaded Monster* destroyed most of Tokyo and almost tolled the death knell for Godzilla, Mothra, and Rodan. And Extraterrestrials tried to abort our space program again (*Frankenstein Meets the Space Monster*).

Facing page:
Aliens possess the dead bodies of Earthian scientists (from **The Invisible Invaders**).

The Cucumber Creature from Venus eyes Beverly Garland when **It Conquered the World**. (AIP).

Just one of the menaces unleashed by **The Teenagers from Outer Space**.

The Cyclopean Mutant carries off Lori Nelson in **World Without End**.

Corcoran has
his hands full
during **Night of the
Blood Beast**.

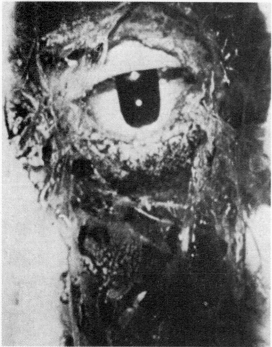

The cyclopean creature that menaced the **Atomic Submarine.**

Earth's first space station is attacked by the indomitable **Green Slime**.

"It!" **The Terror from Beyond Space** eliminates another astronaut.

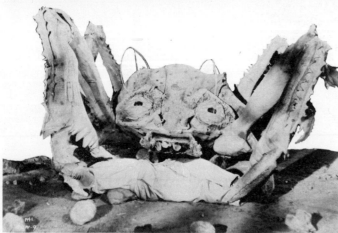

Roger Corman's underrated classic **Attack of the Crab Monsters** is an example of the "Anti-technology"/ "Monster on the Loose" sub genre.

The First Man into Space has returned covered with extraterrestrial goop.

The Space Children and their mentor.

The tentacles of Yog grab an islander to crush him to death in **Yog: Monster from Space**.

On the **Angry Red Planet**, the awesome bat-rat-spider attacks.

Bob Ball is menaced by **The Invasion of the Star Creatures**.

One of **The Teenagers from Outer Space** communicates with an adult from inner space.

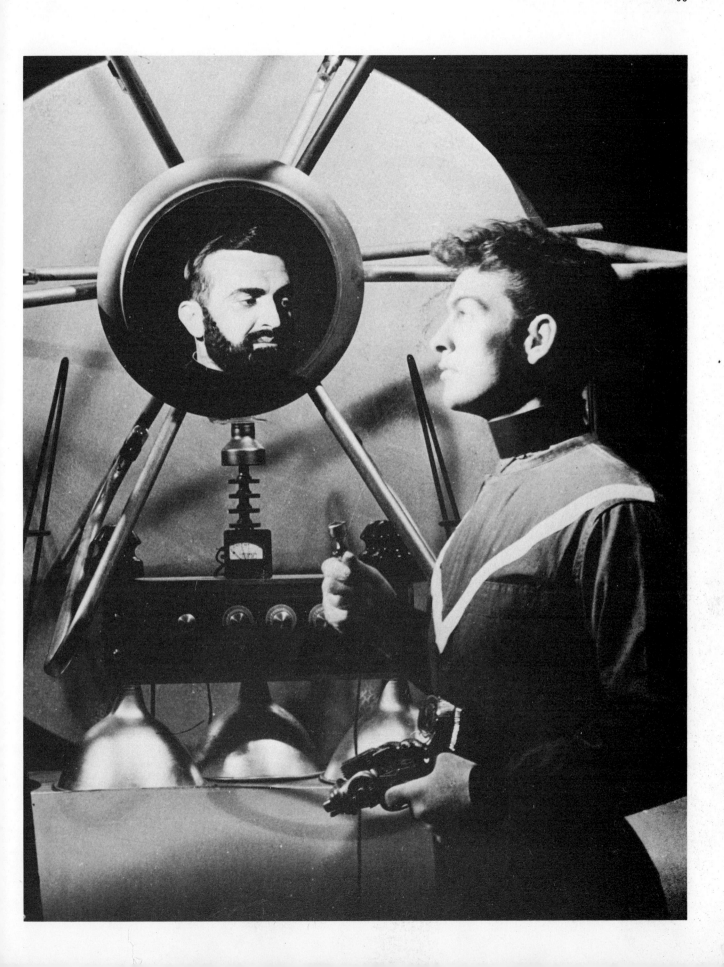

What the intrepid astronauts of 1950s found when they took a **Missile to the Moon**.

Overleaf:
Hans Conreid comes face to face with his possessed T.V. in **The Twonky**.

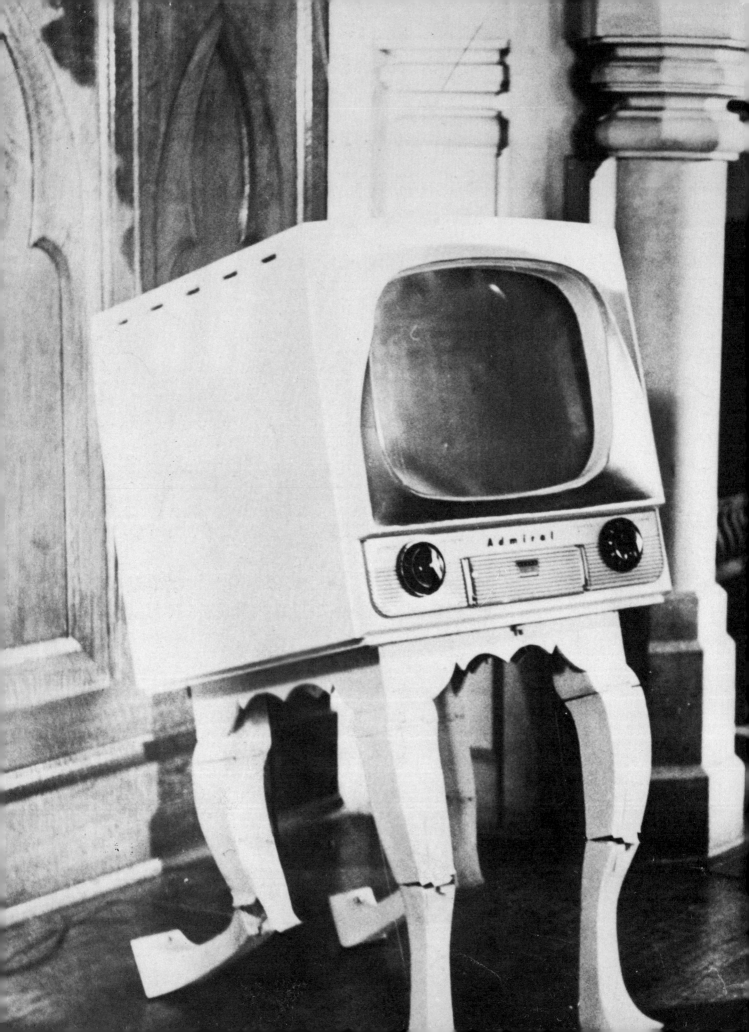

CHAPTER FOUR
GALACTIC ENCOUNTERS

Since time immemorial, Man has wondered, "Are we alone?" And if not, who's out there?" First encounters between Man and extraterrestrials, ET's have been explored since the birth of cinema.

George Méliès' *A Trip to the Moon* visualised concepts and creatures imagined by such writers as Jules Verne and H. G. Wells in a seven-and-a-half-minute seriocomic fantasy. Wells' *First Men in the Moon* was adapted faithfully by the Charles Schneer-Ray Harryhausen team in the early sixties and it illustrated the dangers of biological contamination.

An MGM cinemascope classic took us to the world of Altair IV, a *Forbidden Planet* where the once mighty Krel lived. Technologically and intellectually superior to us, the Krel were destroyed in a single night by the innermost demons of their subconscious.

Extraterrestrial visits to earth has been the theme of several films. When Klaatu came in peace with a gift for the president (so that he could study life on our planet), he was immediately shot by the U.S. Army. Only after *The Day the Earth Stood Still*, was Klaatu able to reveal his mission to Earth. David Bowie was *The Man Who Fell to Earth*, who tried in vain to return to his family on his desert planet only to become a drunken alien sot. Stanley Kubrick's *2001: A Space Odyssey* postulated that man's intelligence is derived from an intergalactic teaching device left on Earth by ET's. Are we descendants of Martian colonists who resemble the devil? (Shades of Clarke's *Childhood's End!*), queries the Hammer films' *Five Million Years to Earth*.

The advent of Steven Spielberg's epic, *Close Encounters of the Third Kind*, in which we communicate peacefully with ET's by means of light and music sees the end of the creeping terrors that have plagued SF films from the outset.

Commander Adams, Doc, and Jerry contemplate a plaster cast of the footprint of the Monster from the Id.

Facing page:
Gort carries Patricia Neal deep into the bowels of the saucer in **The Day the Earth Stood Still**.

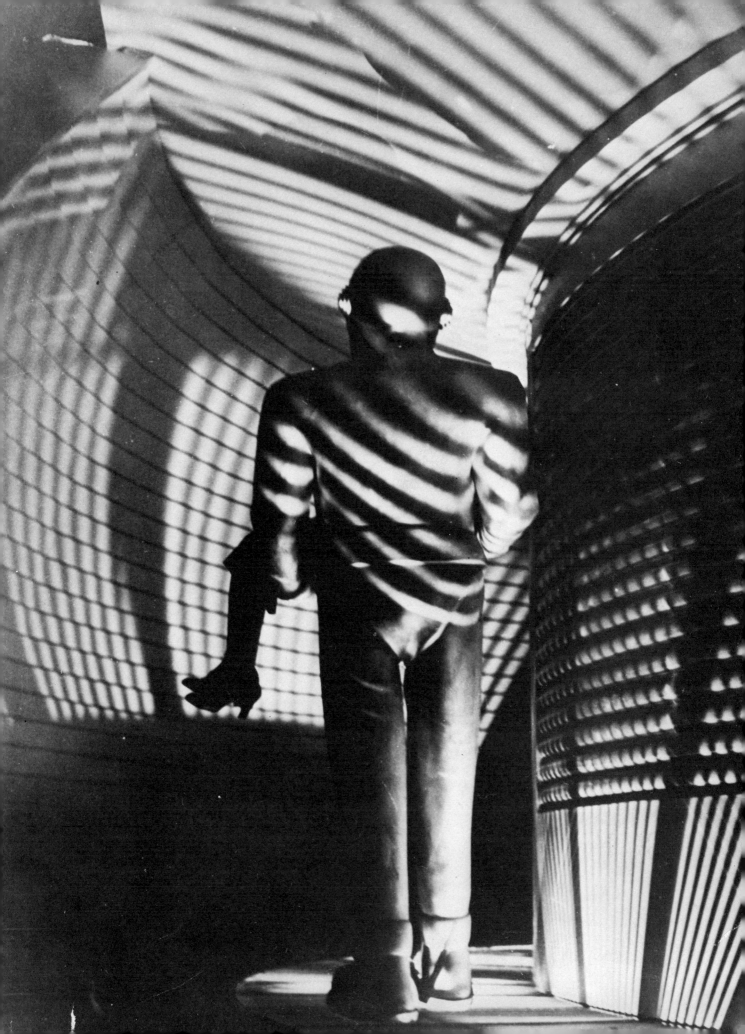

Frame-by-frame visualization of film pioneer Georges Méliès' **A Trip to the Moon** (1902).

Overleaf:
First Men in the Moon cavort on the moon's surface.

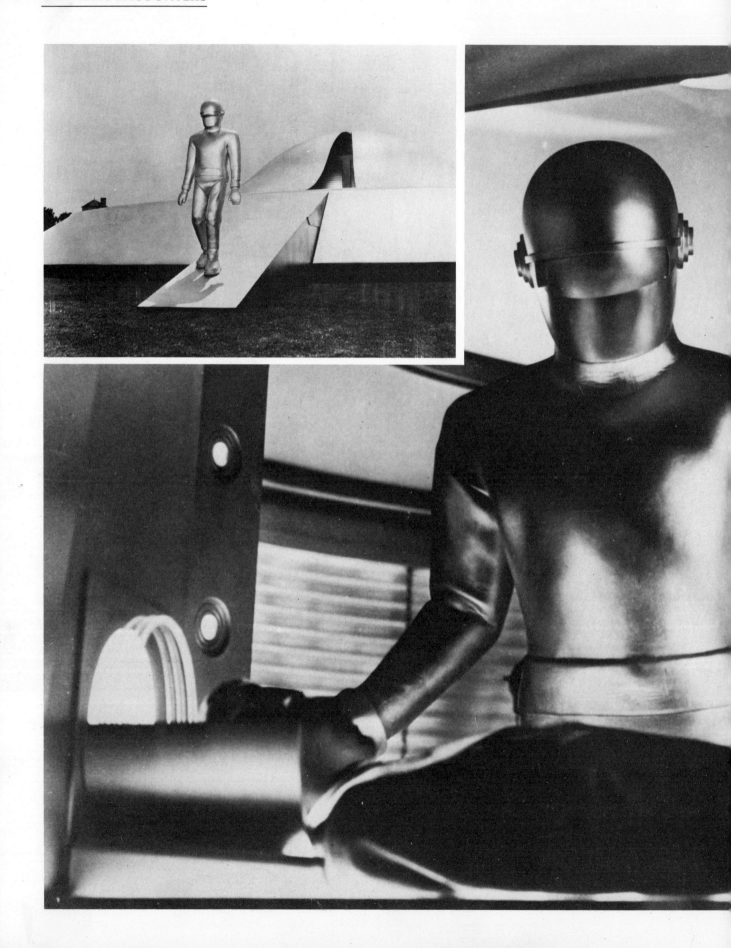

Gort attempts to revive his master.

Dr. Morbius (Walter
Pidgeon) and his
daughter Altaira
(Anne Francis) greet
Commander J. J.
Adams (Leslie
Nielsen) in
Forbidden Planet.

Robbie the Robot
makes a new friend
(Earl Holliman).

Overleaf:
Martha Hyer is
shocked by a
Sélénite at the
window of Cavor's
ship.

113

In Cat-women of the Moon Sonny Tufts discovers a race of Hollywood beauties.

Inside their craft, a martian mutant has Helena Carter safely within its grasp. From **Invaders from Mars.**

Gloria Talbott is the wife
no one believes when she
exclaims **"I Married A
Monster From Outer
Space!"**

When **Robot Monster**
appeared on the bottom
of a triple bill, its
retouched poster stated
that they came from
Mars. Actually, they came
from the dark side of the
moon.

116

The benevolent priest prepares to meet malevolent Martians from George Pal's production of H.G. Wells' classic **War of the Worlds**.

Divine retribution as the Martian from **War of the Worlds** expires.

118

Former President Richard M. Nixon came **From Beyond the Unknown** to confound Jupiter's scientific community. Art by Murphy Anderson.

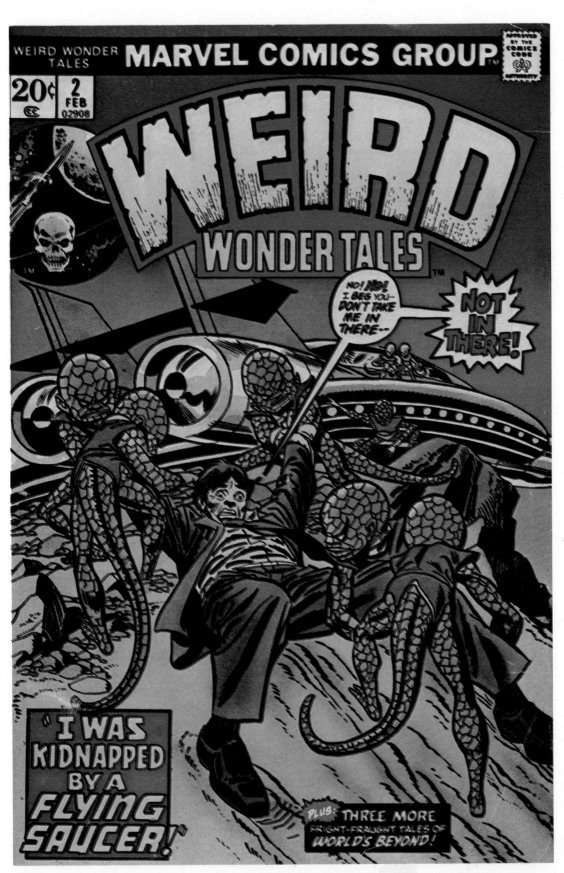

Cover art by Gil Kane and Tom Palmer for a fear fraught tale of flying saucers. From **Weird Wonder Tales** comic magazine.

Overleaf:

Interplanetary cooperation aboard Enterprise.

Captain Kirk is beset with multitudes of Tribbles from the episode **"The Troubles With Tribbles."**

Ruk—The android with no soul.

Captain Kirk must battle the alien commander of a starship in this adaptation of Fredrick Brown's **Arena.**

This white gorilla with horn is a tribute to Flash Gordon's Orangepod.

Creature with large cranial capacity endangers crew of the Enterprise.

Lord Darth Vader from
Lucas' space fantasy
Star Wars.

America's droids,
R2D2 and C3P0, from
Star Wars.

128

Luke Skywalker (Mark Hamill) inspects a droid offered for sale by the mercenary Jawas. From **Star Wars.**

© 1977 Twentieth Century-Fox Film Corporation. All rights reserved.

An Imperial Stormtrooper roams the sands of Tatooine in search of escaped droids in **Star Wars.**

© 1977 Twentieth Century-Fox Film Corporation. All rights reserved.

Professor
Quatermass (Andrew
Keir) inspects the
remains of a long-
dead Martian in
Hammer's **Five
Million Years to
Earth**.

129

In the course of the film, David Bowie reverts from a Christ figure to a drunken alien sot.

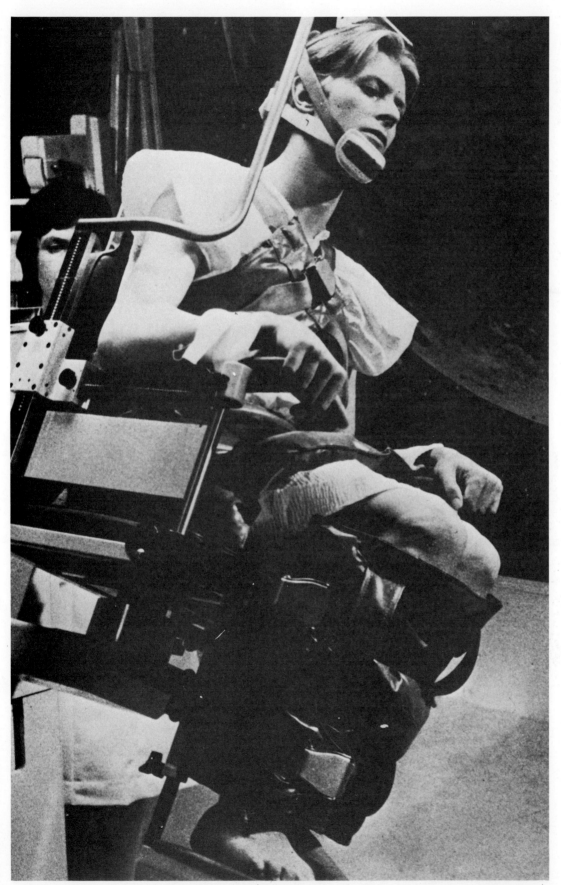

David Bowie as
Thomas Jerome
Newton, an alien
astronaut who
attempts to return
to his world of origin
in **The Man Who Fell
to Earth**.

A bizarre dragon-like creature from **La Planète Sauvage** (Fantastic Planet)

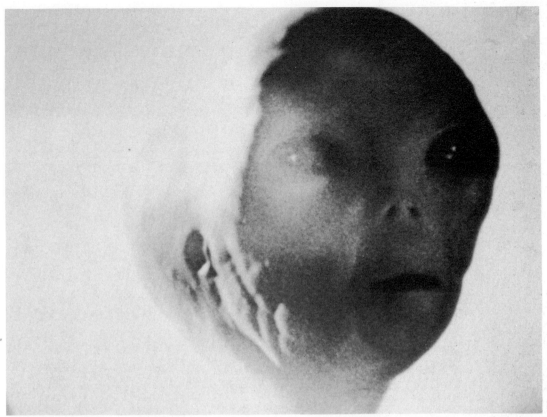

Facing page:
James Earl Jones as Barney Hill, finds himself on an interrupted journey.

The leader of the UFO beams with pride as Roy Neary (Richard Dreyfuss) prepares to board the Mother ship in **Close Encounters of the Third Kind.**

CHAPTER FIVE
TUBE ALIENS

Since the infancy of television, alien creatures of all types have slithered across the screen. *Rocky Jones, Space Ranger* kept the interstellar void free of alien vermin. George Reeves will always be remembered as that champion of truth, justice, and the American way, when he ditched his glasses and press pass and became *Superman*. Syndication has kept the indestructible Man of Steel in public view since the show's inception in the mid-fifties.

Rod Serling, creator, producer, principal writer, and host of *The Twilight Zone* brought literate SF to home viewers. Tales of space zoos, new worlds, robots and aliens were often adapted from the works of mainstream SF writers like Charles Beaumont and Ray Bradbury. Serling's scripts often contained that O. Henry twist ending that was to become the trademark of *Twilight Zone*.

Irwin Allen's classic space opera, *Lost in Space*, featured an incredible menagerie of juvenile aliens intent on keeping the Robinson family lost. Eventually, the Robot, Dr. Smith Will and the *Whatizit* of the week became the stars of the series.

Joseph Stefano's *The Outer Limits* had an alien or creature every week. The scripts were intelligent and suspenseful, and the effects team, which included Jim (*Jack the Giant Killer*) Danforth and Wah (*Flesh Gordon*) Chang, was continually creating and animating imaginative ET's.

Star Trek attained even greater heights of popularity after its demise. *Trek* included gangsters, Nazis, Indians, Romans, and the insipid Yangs (Yankees) and Coms (Communists), in worlds that would "mysteriously" duplicate Earth's history.

Facing page:
Rod Serling, creator and host of television's celebrated science-fiction fantasy series **The Twilight Zone,** finds himself in heaven.

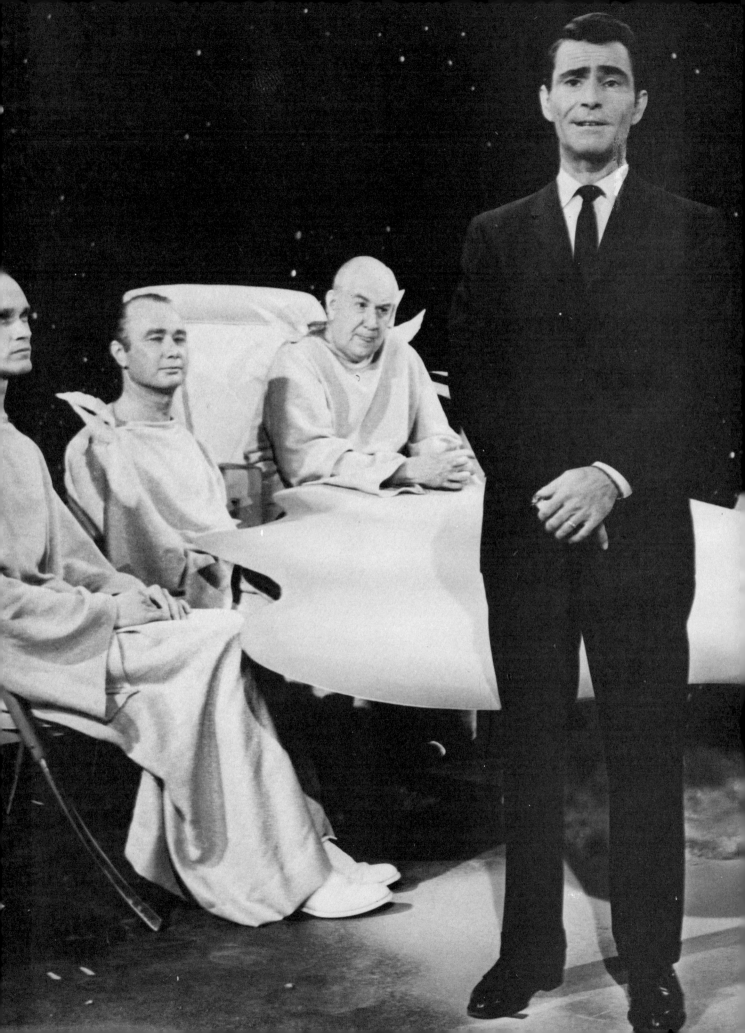

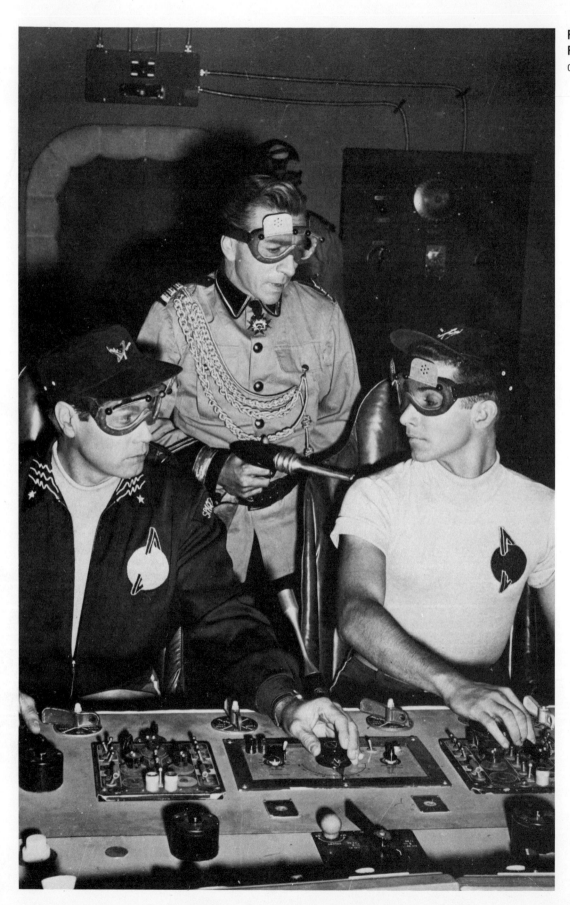

Rocky Jones, Space Ranger at the mercy of a Mercurian.

Superman (George
Reeves) aids one of the
tiny visitors from the
earth's core in the
episode, **Superman and
the Mole Man.**

Overleaf:
Superman (George
Reeves) metes out
justice to criminals.

Mrs. Robinson (June Lockhart) is menaced by yet another creature (from **Lost in Space**).

Right:
Smith in the grips of **The Golden Man**.

Tybo (Stanley Adams) an intelligent carrot accuses Dr. Smith of murdering plants when he picks some posies for the Robot's birthday celebration.

Overleaf:
Gary Conway and Don Matheson struggle to free their comrade before a giant entomologist returns (from **Land of the Giants**).

A close encounter between two alien civilizations on **Lost in Space**.

William Shatner cannot believe his senses when he encounters "The Nightmare at 20,000 Feet" from **The Twilight Zone.**

Michael (**Day the Earth Stood Still**) Rennie starred as **The Keeper** who wished to keep Will and Penny for his intergalactic space zoo. (from **Lost in Space**).

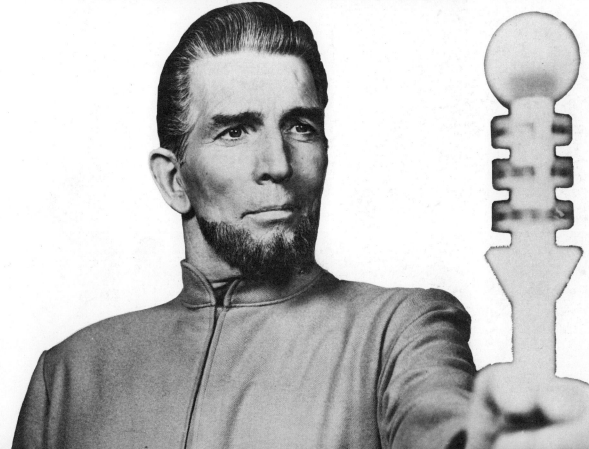

David McCallum in
"The Sixth Finger"
episode of Joseph
Stefanos' **The Outer
Limits**.

Ray Walston as
Uncle Martin in the
long running
teleseries, **My
Favorite Martian**.

TUBE ALIENS

The ever-popular
Coneheads from
**NBC's Saturday
Night Live** (from left
to right, Larraine
Newman, Elliot
Gould, Jane Curtin,
and Dan Aykroyd).

A pulp-inspired
creature (Martin
Landau) from **The
Outer Limits**.

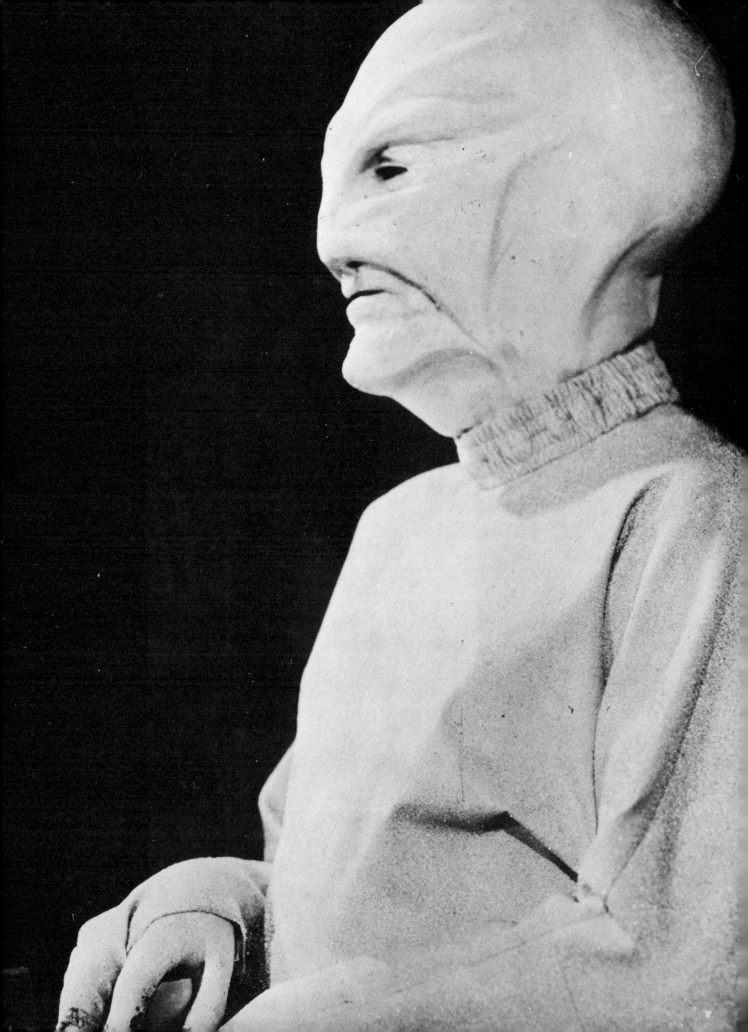

All the classic forms of aliens are prevalent in **Space: 1999** including those with large cranial capacities.

A scientist from the future (Peter Cushing).

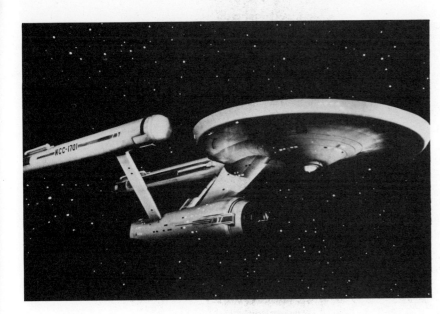

The starship Enterprise from television's most popular science-fiction series, **Star Trek**.

Captain Kirk (William Shatner) battles Ruk, the synthetic android (Ted Cassidy) in the episode "What Are Little Girls Made Of?"

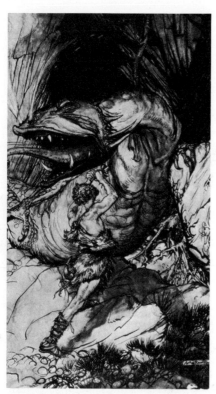

Siegfried, the
mythological warrior
of Germany, slays
Fafner, the dragon in
this painting by
noted fantasy
illustrator, Arthur
Rackham.

AFTERWORD

It is hazardous to predict the future of the science-fiction film, since the medium, like its literary cousin, is inextricably linked with the development of science itself. Films like *Destination: Moon* are already hopelessly dated, and a remake of *The War of the Worlds* will have to pick a planet other than Mars as the alien home world. But I suggest that in general science-fiction films, especially those concerning extraterrestrials, will develop along two interdependent lines. We can expect to see the technology of the film medium itself increasingly celebrated, as it has been in effects extravaganzas like *2001: A Space Odyssey, Star Wars* and *Close Encounters of the Third Kind*. At the same time—and I am perhaps ascribing more intellectual curiosity to Hollywood than is entirely justifiable—we will hopefully see a deepening sophistication about the nature of the cosmos and its hypothetical non-human residents, which will provide worthy subject matter upon which to lavish the technological treasure chest available to the film maker.

Lucas and Spielberg typify a new breed of science-fiction film maker (though of course they do not limit their efforts to this type of film alone). Young by Hollywood standards, they grew up in the NASA age and saw the flourishing of science-fiction literature from pulp adventure to the only form of fiction which today seriously asks questions of a philosophic nature: who are we, where did we come from, and are we alone? It can be reliably expected that film makers of the Lucas-Spielberg generation will continue to answer the last question with a resounding no. It is to be hoped that they will apply the serious criteria of science-fiction literature, as did Kubrick in collaborating with the distinguished novelist Arthur C. Clarke on *2001*, to the treatment of their alien beings.

However, the film maker who wishes to present screen aliens as provocative and fascinating as those of recent science-fiction literature runs into an obstacle—the nature of the film medium itself. In a written story, suggestion and ambiguity are powerful tools: writing is an abstract art form dealing in concepts, and no matter how naturalistically a writer sets down his description, the picture it summons up will differ from one reader's mind to another's. A case in point: to fantasy fans J. R. R. Tolkien's epic trilogy *The Lord of the Rings* is a touchstone not least because of the strange creatures who enrich its pages. Yet efforts to depict the Elves, Hobbits, Dwarves, Orcs and Dragons of the book, either in paintings or in animated cartoons, have almost universally disappointed the trilogy's readership. Why? Because they represent only one artist's (in the case of the Hildebrandts, two) visualization. One opinion cannot possibly encompass the variety of images that dance behind the eyes of several million readers when they read Tolkien's haunting descriptions. Literature, then, is suggestive, whereas film deals in the concrete. The film maker must make a decision about what will actually appear on the screen, and all the sophistries of filters, mattework, cutaways and fancy dissolves cannot save him from the moment when his medium demands he Show and Tell.

Sinbad slays the dragon servant of the evil wizard Sokurah in the **Seventh Voyage of Sinbad**.

Sparked by alien intervention (The Monolith), man begins his ascent.

AFTERWORD

It can be suggested that the hard literality of the film medium makes it ideal for documentary work and inadequate, ultimately, for the sort of suggestive lyricism that finds its most extreme expression in science fiction and fantasy. Certainly, as long as the film maker is lovingly panning his literal eye over the complex solidities of a spacecraft whose design is based on careful extrapolation from NASA reality, he is on safe ground. It is no wonder that the most recent science-fiction films have appealed to the public primarily because of their documentary recording of wonderful technology.

But science fiction is not simply about technology. In the purist sense of the term, it is about hardware's effect on software—and the software is not necessarily human. There is a careful description of an alien life-form in the fine novel *The Mote in God's Eye,* by Larry Niven and Jerry Pournelle. Details—number of limbs, musculature, skeletal structure, piliation, coloring, locomotion, etc.—accumulate on the page until the reader has formed a fascinating image of the alien in his mind. Moreover, like all conscientious science-fiction writers, the team has gone to some pains to create a creature that could conceivably "work." That is, they have limited the "what if" factor to what is possible insofar as we understand the boundaries of anatomy and physiology and the imperatives of chemistry.

Yet the "Moties," as they are called in the novel, remain tantalizingly mysterious. We have been told about them, but the seeing is left up to the reader. We know how they move, but it is up to us to animate them. We are given room by the very nature of the written word to speculate, and since any description of an extraterrestrial must remain speculative until one arrives here in the flesh, the writers have done their job handsomely. Suspending disbelief is easy, in the the novel: we can "see" the Moties with our mind's eye as easily as we can "see" the human characters—whose existence in written form, like that of the aliens, is conceptual not actual.

Bring both humans and Moties to the screen, however, and there is an immediate problem. The humans will be real men and women; actors who are only portraying star ship crews, but still palpably and demonstrably human. The Moties, however, will necessarily be constructions—either animated models or humans in alien suits—whose only "reality" is their self-evident artificiality.

In this sense, Kubrick and Clarke made a wiser choice than did Spielberg in not showing their aliens on the screen. Spielberg's film, honest and searching as it was, in a sense fell apart at the moment when the dazzling light playing around the door of the mother ship dimmed slightly to reveal what was only too apparently a clever animated model. In short, it was impossible to accept the reality of the alien with the same intensity with which we had been sharing in the lives of the sweating, smiling, suffering and ecstatic human characters in the film, and the disparity injured the film's climax.

An example of Alex Raymond's incredible draftsmanship for **Flash Gordon.**

AFTERWORD

There is another reason why the science-fiction film will continue to fall short of the imaginative achievements of serious science-fiction literature: Money. Compared to the costs of putting out even as inexpensive a film as *Invasion of the Body Snatchers,* the production of a science-fiction novel, magazine or collection of short stories is cheap. There is an old show-biz saying to the effect that art is what closes in New Haven, and, fortunately, like most old saws it isn't strictly true. Nonetheless, the science-fiction writers and their editors will continue to enjoy a much wider leeway for the introduction of hard (read "intellectually challenging") science and hard (ditto) thought into their entertainments, simply because the financial stakes involved don't even approach those attendant upon a major commercial film.

Science-fiction film makers absolutely must assure themselves of a large audience for their product before they even begin production. Simply to break even a *Star Wars* must show seven figures at the box office within a very few weeks of its premiere, and producers don't make pictures just to break even. This means that if a film maker wishes to make a film dealing with a subtle "think" subject from science-fiction literature, unless he is a con man and can charm the birds from the trees he will have to resign himself to a relatively cheap and shoddy production—thereby denying himself the special effects that are the chief joy of the science-fiction movie. Few investors are willing to risk money on anything that puts a demand on the audience beyond the consumption of the popcorn.

On the other hand, big money will always be available to the sharp science-fiction producer who can dazzle an audience with his technological footwork—but in choosing his subject, he will have to operate within the arbitrary guidelines dictated by Hollywood's often wrongheaded analyses of past "successes."

Hence, the science-fiction film will continue to trot out stale issues. *Star Wars* is self-evidently the Buck Rogers serial of the '70s. *Superman* is currently in production. Even *Close Encounters of the Third Kind* is based on a pastiche of old concepts that have been thoroughly market-tested to assure their popularity and iced with a thin layer of jingoistic Americanism that would do a Joe McCarthy proud.

If this last remark seems to stand at variance with what I have said earlier about the general excellence of the film, let me qualify it somewhat. I approve of Spielberg's attempt to deal forthrightly with the Otherness of his extraterrestrials. Here are no idealized human beings in funny clothes, or ravening sentient rutabagas. His aliens are believably Other in their powers, motives and relationships with human beings (why in the Universe did they want to capture an entire Naval Air Squadron, planes and all?). But every bizarre UFO sighting comes from the annals of "actual" UFO encounters, and his alien beings represent the two physical types most often reported in UFOlogy, that most whimsical of pseudosciences. Already Spielberg is assured of a mass audience composed of readers of the *National Enquirer* and the folks who believe little green men are transmitting messages in Morse

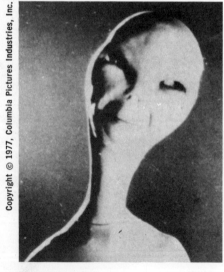

The amiable alien ambassador from **Close Encounters of the Third Kind.**

code through the fillings of their teeth. And in the America of the late '70s that audience is on the increase, for reasons obvious to anyone who watches the TV evening news.

Being a believer myself—if not in my fillings as cosmic radio stations, at least in the possibility of extraterrestrial life—I don't grudge the science-fiction film makers their reliance on tested box-office grabbers based on analysis of the types of things the UFO believers think they've seen. But the idea that star-traveling beings of illimitable power and wisdom elect to land only in the United States, that they are willing to deal with a U.S. Government agency whose virulent paranoia is tempered only slightly by the mocking attitude Spielberg displays toward it, that the astronauts—with the exception of Richard Dreyfuss—picked by the aliens for humankind's first voyage of cosmic enlightenment are NASA androids right down to the American flags on the shoulders of their jumpsuits—are all insults to the intelligence, if not of the human audience for the film, then of the aliens. That audiences seem entirely content with the film so far, as they have been generally happy with filmdom's previous attempts to capture the mystery that lies around the subject of first contact since the day the first actor climbed into a cardboard freak suit and carried off a nubile Earth girl, should be sufficient reason to show what a tough row the science-fiction film maker still has to hoe if he wishes to rival the spiritual and intellectual stimulation afforded by his literary opposite numbers. Reading, after all, demands the ability to conceptualize. The film image's direct impact upon the visual centers of the cortex is not so demanding.

However, aliens in science-fiction movies have grown up along with their creators. Simplistic remakes of the serials of the '30s and '40s are no longer possible without considerable injections of camp (*Wonder Woman*, q.v.). *Star Wars* is, after all, a far subtler movie than the Flash Gordon series, though Luke Skywalker and Han Solo are Flash's grandchildren. The video age has created a generation of technology-wise people who cannot be content with complacent assurances that Our Kind and Our Machines will always prevail. The age of the monster and the blue-eyed hero has been swallowed up by the real complexities of real technology, and technology has pointed the way to new adventures in time and space in which intelligence, sympathy and an appreciation of the wondrous variety of life will prove far more important than a quick finger on the trigger of a Matter Disorganizer.

Martin the Martian returns to bedevil Bugs Bunny. Martin also made a cameo in Spielberg's **Close Encounters of the Third Kind**.

As our troubled human community stumbles toward a recognition of its common plight as uneasy riders of the little space ship Earth, we must eventually arrive at humility when we attempt to conceive of cultures that have matured enough to master the problems—spiritual as well as technical—besetting us. Science-fiction films have arrived at a crossroads. They can continue to soothe the public with traditional idiocies about the cosmos and its inhabitants, tricked up with light shows and brain-bending sound effects. Or they can utilize their technological facilities in an attempt to capture the sense of joyful and, in a real sense, religious wonder that informs the best of the science-fiction writers when they contemplate the infinitude of the possible under a clear night sky.

Acknowledgements

The authors would like to thank the following, without whose hard work and patience this book would have been impossible.

Ben Bova, Jill Carin, Marc Corcoran, Bob Ghiraldini, Sam Griffin, Ken Kleppert, Tom Kowal, Ric Meyers, Jerry Ohlinger, Terry Ork, Jeff Rovin, Bernie Schleifer, Joe Theodorescu, Stephen C. Wathen, and Susan Willmarth. Special thanks also to Our Man from Aldebaran, Y't-aaer 314.

Credits

Academy Film Stills Archive: pp. 2L, 6, 17T, 19, 23, 24, 31, 51, 52-53, 54-55, 56TB, 57, 58TB, 59TB, 70T, 74-75, 76B, 85, 86, 90B, 96-97, 100, 101, 106-107, 108-109, 138, 142B, 143, 146, 189, 155T.
Cinemabilia: 4-5, 5, 17B, 21, 62-63, 72TB, 76T, 87T, 112, 129, 144-145.
Howard Frank: From the photo collection of Howard Frank, Personality Photos, Inc., P.O. Box 50, Brooklyn, N.Y. 11230: 137, 139, 147T.

Ohlinger's: 1LR, 3, 4, 14, 45, 64B, 77, 79B, 80T, 87B, 111, 112B, 113TB, 114, 115, 130, 134, 148, 150, 151, 152LR, 153TB, 159.
Jeff Rovin: 2R, 61B, 65, 90T.
Stephen C. Wathen: 78TB, 79T, 80B, 155B.

We wish to credit the following for film and other material used:

Above Average Productions, Inc.: p. 150.   Allied Artists, Inc.: 36L, 37, 44T, 72TB, 90B.
American International Pictures: 76TB, 86, 87B, 88-89. Astor Films: 96-97.
Edgar Rice Burroughs, Inc., Tarzana, California: 19.
CBS: 137, 142TB, 143, 146, 146TB, 149.
Cinema Five, Inc.: 130, 131.
Columbia Pictures: 1L, 2R, 4-5, 14, 28, 32, 38, 61T, 62-63, 106-107, 155T, 158.
Condé Nast: 42LR, 43, 47, 78TB, 79TB, 112, 135TB.
D. C. Comics: 61TB, 118, 139, 140-141.
Prado Museum, Madrid (Francisco Goya, Saturn): 11.

Colmer Museum (Matthias Grünewald, The Temptation of St. Anthony, detail from the Isenheim Altar): 12.

ITC Entertainment, Ltd.: 152LR.

Janus Films: Used by permission of Janus Films, Inc.: 29.

King Features: Courtesy King Features Syndicate: 157.
Mammoth Films: Copyright © Mammoth Films, Inc., 1974: 64B.
Marvel Comics Group: 119.

MGM: From the MGM release The Green Slime, © 1968, Metro-Goldwyn-Mayer Incorporated: 90T.

From the MGM release Forbidden Planet, © 1956, Loew's Incorporated: 25, 36R.

From the MGM release 2001: A Space Odyssey, © 1968, Metro-Goldwyn-Mayer Incorporated: 7, 21, 155B.
New World Pictures: 132-133.
Paramount Pictures: 33B, 61B, 65, 77, 80TB, 81, 82-83, 116, 116-117, 120, 121, 122 (both), 124, 125, 153TB.
RKO: Courtesy of RKO General Pictures: 70B, 71TB.
"Siegfried Kills Fafnir," illustration by Arthur Rackham for Siegfried and the Twilight of the Gods, William Heineman, 1911.: 154. Reed Productions: 138.   Republic Pictures International: 60.
Twentieth Century-Fox Film Corporation: 2L, 18, 23, 34, 35, 48 (both), 73, 103, 108-109, 129, 144-145.   United Artists Corporation: 1R, 3, 74-75, 85, 91, 98-99, 100, 148, 151.

Universal Pictures: From the motion picture The Andromeda Strain, 17B. Frankenstein, 10. It Came From Outer Space, 15, 17T, 69. This Island Earth, 4, 30, 31, 75. The UFO Incident, 134.
Warner Brothers: 87T, 159.
Warren Publications: 33T.
Wade Williams Productions: 44B.

DATE DUE

47970